Goldendoodle

Series "Fun Facts on Dogs for Kids"

Written by Michelle Hawkins

Goldendoodle

Series "Fun Facts on Dogs for Kids"

By: Michelle Hawkins

Version 1.1 ~February 2021

Published by Michelle Hawkins at KDP

Copyright ©2021 by Michelle Hawkins. All rights reserved.

No part of this publication may be reproduced, distributed or transmitted in any form or by any means including photocopying, recording or other electronic or mechanical methods or by any information storage or retrieval system without the prior written permission of the publishers, except in the case of very brief quotations embodied in critical reviews and certain other noncommercial uses permitted by copyright law.

All rights reserved, including the right of reproduction in whole or in part in any form.

All information in this book has been carefully researched and checked for factual accuracy. However, the author and publisher make no warranty, express or implied, that the information contained herein is appropriate for every individual, situation, or purpose and assume no responsibility for errors or omissions.

The reader assumes the risk and full responsibility for all actions. The author will not be held responsible for any loss or damage, whether consequential, incidental, special or otherwise, that may result from the information presented in this book.

All images are free for use or purchased from stock photo sites or royalty-free for commercial use. I have relied on my own observations as well as many different sources for this book, and I have done my best to check facts and give credit where it is due. In the event that any material is used without proper permission, please contact me so that the oversight can be corrected.

Goldendoodles are a mix of a Golden Retriever and a Poodle.

Goldendoodles are known to be great with children.

The fur on a Goldendoodle can be curly, straight, or wavy.

Goldendoodles are considered a mixed breed of dogs.

Goldendoodles are very intelligent.

Goldendoodles enjoy learning and playing fetch and frisbee.

Goldendoodles can be hypoallergenic, but no guarantees.

Goldendoodles enjoy socializing with both pets and humans.

The Goldendoodles are not an aggressive breed.

Training and socialization early are what is best for Goldendoodles.

Goldendoodles are a quiet dog.

Due to the mix, Goldendoodles are very intelligent.

The average age span for a Goldendoodles is between ten to fifteen years

Goldendoodles are very obedient.

Every Goldendoodle is different; no two are alike.

As puppies, Goldendoodles are easy to train.

Goldendoodles are friendly to everyone.

Other names for Goldendoodles are Golden Poos, Goldie Poos, or Groodles.

Goldendoodles are lively.

Goldendoodles do not make a good guard dog.

Goldendoodles are known to be friendly with all animals.

Goldendoodles are considered a designer dog.

Goldendoodles are very gentle

In competitions, Goldendoodles do well.

Goldendoodles make excellent guide dogs.

Brushing the Goldendoodles coat twice a week is ideal.

Goldendoodles enjoy cuddling with their family.

Goldendoodles are very gentle.

The miniature Goldendoodle is between thirteen to twenty inches.

The weight of a miniature Goldendoodles is between fifteen to thirty-five pounds.

Goldendoodles are easy to train.

It would be best if you wiped the ears on your Goldendoodle regularly to avoid ear infections.

Goldendoodles are very lovable.

Goldendoodles love the company of others.

When you hear your Goldendoodles click their nails on the floor, it is time for them to be trimmed.

Goldendoodles enjoy learning new tricks.

Goldendoodles come in a variety of colors.

Goldendoodles make great companions for seniors and nursing home residents.

Goldendoodles are very empathetic.

If left alone for long periods of time, Goldendoodles can have separation anxiety.

Goldendoodles are very open to strangers.

Goldendoodles are very playful.

The coat on a Goldendoodle sheds very little.

The short hair on Goldendoodles is more manageable.

Goldendoodles are known to train and learn fast.

Goldendoodles are eager to please everyone.

Goldendoodles are not considered to be a hyper dog.

If you have the time, Goldendoodles are a natural at dog shows.

Toys are considered an outlet for your Goldendoodles energy and curiosity.

Goldendoodles are known to enjoy hiking and the outdoors.

Goldendoodles need thirty to sixty minutes of exercise daily.

If strangers approach, Goldendoodles will not bark.

Goldendoodles can read your mood and act accordingly.

Goldendoodles started in the United States and Australia.

The teeth on a Goldendoodle need to be cleaned two to three times a week.

Goldendoodles are known to be very athletic.

Goldendoodles are considered intelligent.

The medium size Goldendoodles are between seventeen to twenty inches in height.

The medium size Goldendoodles average weight is between forty to fifty pounds.

Goldendoodles do not like being left alone.

A common problem for Goldendoodles is food allergies.

Always show affection to your Goldendoodles.

Goldendoodles are very friendly.

The standard Goldendoodles heigh is between twenty to twenty-four inches.

The standard Goldendoodle average weight is between fifty to ninety pounds.

Goldendoodles make excellent therapy dogs.

Goldendoodles have a high level of curiosity.

Playing often with your Goldendoodles helps with boredom.

Little barking will come out of your Goldendoodle.

The coat on a Goldendoodle will get lighter as they age.

Goldendoodles enjoy long walks with their owners.

Goldendoodles make great search and rescue dogs.

Goldendoodles are known to be lazy as well as active.

Goldendoodles make great companions for the elderly.

Goldendoodles enjoy games of chase.

Goldendoodles do best in a yard with a fenced-in backyard to allow them to run.

Goldendoodles are very loyal to their family.

Goldendoodles make great guide dogs for the blind.

Goldendoodles are always up for an adventure and seeing the world.

By giving Goldendoodles treats, it encourages proper training.

Goldendoodles are known to love to swim.

Goldendoodles will listen well because they want to please their owner.

Goldendoodles enjoy large families; more loving and playing.

Goldendoodles thrive with a steady routine and environment.

Goldendoodles love the spotlight on them.

Find me on Amazon at:

https://amzn.to/3oqoXoG

and on Facebook at:

https://bit.ly/3ovFJ5V

Other Books by Michelle Hawkins

Series

Fun Facts on Birds for Kids.

Fun Fact on Fruits and Vegetables

Fun Facts on Small Animals

Fun Facts on Dogs for Kids.

Made in the USA
Monee, IL
31 October 2021